Audacity

MEMOIRS OF TRANSITIONING

Audacity

MEMOIRS OF TRANSITIONING

M. GREG GREEN

ISBN 978-1-7349987-0-2

Table of Contents

"Finding yourself isn't hard,
the courage to actually be yourself is."

M. Greg Green

Dedication

In memory of Grandpa Dewey
who encouraged me with these words:

"You know why they don't like you? Because
you have the audacity to be yourself."

W. Dewey Tullis

Acknowledgments

I wouldn't be at this place in life without my beautiful wife Tamara. Thank you for always encouraging me to do what's on my heart. Everyone needs someone like you in their corner, and I am so grateful to have you in mine.

Thank you to my father who took a risk as a single dad raising me. You have stayed on this journey with me, even when we didn't know where it was going.

Thank you Grandma Kittie for always being yourself- blunt and full of colorful words, which always make me laugh.

To Doretta and Herman, thank you for allowing me the honor of carrying your mother's name.

Two simple words, "I care." Those words made the difference in life and death- literally. Thank you, Rebecca, for saving my life, I am forever grateful.

To all the teachers who got to watch me grow up and change and stood by me, thank you.

To my professors who pushed me to be better, especially Colonel James A.W. Rembert, thank you.

To the former cadet who said I would never finish, "his school," thank you for motivating me. I hope your getting kicked out for an honor violation was as beneficial to molding your adulthood as me graduating "my school" molded mine.

To my mentor, Ronda Dean, you motivated me before we truly knew the path of our relationship.

To the most spiritual woman I know, who embodies the golden rule of treating others how you want to be treated, Velvet. You took care of me when I needed a place to run and all these years later, your door is still open.

To Paul, when everyone else turned their backs on me, you were still there. Even without the badge, you make me feel like I still belong to the team, thank you.

To Ms. Courtenay, I was too embarrassed to ask for help. You allowed me into your home for almost a year while I worked out my life. I will forever be thankful!

To my Tau Kappa Phi, Inc. phamily, especially Senia, Marlene, Gayle, Que, and Cameron. Senia you taught me how to let loose and have fun in life. Marlene, you taught me how to keep my game face on through all the chaos of the world. Gayle, Que, and Cameron you all have had my back to the end and exemplify what it means to be a TRUE KANE!

To Ashlee, I thank you. You guided me through the early stages of my transition. From truly acknowledging who I was to finding, the best top surgeon in the country, you are much appreciated.

To all of my transgender siblings who have helped me to and through my journey, and to those who trusted in me to help you through yours, I thank you. You give me purpose and energy to keep fighting for us.

Introduction

Being bold and being yourself, can be the biggest acts of bravery, or so I'm told. On one hand, I understand that being a black transgender man in the South is an act of bravery. Let's be real, the South has never been a fan of black men. So it has definitely been an eye-opening gut check to walk the streets as the man I am today. On the other hand, I don't see how anyone can continue living a life where they don't feel complete. As the world continues to show us how short life is, why wouldn't you want to be as happy as possible?

In some ways, being bold can be considered selfish. For family and friends who didn't know how to respond to my choices, this could have been how they viewed my new attitude. As I became more comfortable in my own skin, I didn't take some of the same nonsense I did in the past.

Before my transition, I was so worried about staying in my lane, that I would let others dictate the actions I would take.

When I started to stand up for myself, I was told my transition was changing me too much and I was being selfish.

As obstacles are thrown in your way, it's important how you deal with them. There are some people who leave home to transition, with less stress from their known environment. Staying home, staying in the same area I grew up in, and working with the same people during my transition, was clearly an act of bravery. I had the audacity to be me in front of everyone! There were times I was terrified, angry, sad, and depressed. After all that happened, I decided to be happy.

We all go through various seasons in life. Sometimes, we get knocked off our path and have to make a decision on what's next. It's not always easy but if you stay true to yourself, you can't go wrong. You can choose to run away from your situation, but in the end, you will still be there, unable to run from your own thoughts. Take a trip with me through the growth and development of my gender identity.

1

IDENTITY

There seemed to be so much confusion about the dynamics of my family. My family was like the Brady Bunch except each parent had only one child. It's as if people didn't fully understand the concept of step-parents or siblings, so that's how I would explain it. Living in a house full of natural charisma mixed with constant sarcasm, I absorbed all I could.

My father, a disc jockey and radio personality, always had a smile on his face. I would go to work with him and imitate his radio voice. Even when he got a studio in the house, I would do the same thing, oftentimes messing up an actual recording. My stepmother, I believe a 3rd generation college graduate, was a teacher and very quick-witted. She had an answer for anyone at any time and it was filled with sarcasm. My stepbrother was the creative one. He was always involved in school plays, played an instrument or danced. He was good at anything with the arts. These were the personalities that made up my household. We became a family when I was about three-years-old. My biological mother, who was from Panama, lived near Atlanta. I didn't know much about her growing up. What I knew was that my father fought for me in court because he knew he could be a better provider for me than she could. She wasn't a citizen and was possibly going to be deported back to Panama. So for the first few years of my life, it was me and my dad.

I was always curious about my Panamanian family, but my stepmother once told me, "There are two types of people in Panama, really rich and really poor. Which do you think you belong to?" This was confusing for me because I didn't know any "rich," or "poor," people. Looking back, I would say I grew up middle class, so I didn't have a concept of the two extremes. Anytime my biological mother would call the house to speak to me, there would be tension.

Speaking to my biological mother made me feel guilty, as if I was doing something wrong. Negative energy that didn't come from my father, but from my stepmom. It was as if she was angry with me for wanting to know where I come from. I remember my step brother's father would call and he and my father would actually have conversations on the phone before passing it on. That courtesy was not given to me and as I grew up it continued to drive a wedge between me and both my mothers.

My stepbrother and I, along with a family friend, used to make videos growing up. Music videos, action videos where we would pretend to be Power Rangers, or imitate other movies. In our house, the kitchen sink had a window that went to a living room area. It was an old carport that had been closed in. We would jump from that window onto a couch making our action films. We would record all day, using old over the shoulder camcorders, and start/stop recording as edits. We had a blast!

When we recorded music videos, I always did a rap and the other two would sing a song. I knew I couldn't sing and I wanted to be a rapper like Lisa "Left-eye" Lopez of the all-female group, TLC. Although we did all of this, my stepbrother and I never seemed to connect with one another. We went to school, were in the band, and did so many things together, but it all seemed superficial.

My father was complicated to me. He used to say to me that blood is thicker than water. No matter what was going on in life, he reassured me that he would always be in my corner, and it was the two of us forever. Before he got married, I remember riding with him early in the mornings to, what I'm assuming was, daycare. He worked the morning show on the radio, so I had to be cared for early in the day. I can see it clearly even today, he had a small white convertible and we would see the sunrise as we rode down the street.

It didn't make much sense to me that he would always speak of it being the two of us since we were now a family of four, as things started to develop, it would become more clear. He and my stepmother were becoming distant. We took family trips to New York, Walt Disney World, Myrtle Beach, and Washington, DC. My father always said the plan was to take a trip every year, and then one year we didn't go anywhere.

I didn't think much of it until we didn't go anywhere as a family at all. That year, all the trips became only school or work-related, and we either went with one parent or separate. At one point, we all went to different places across the country. My stepmom flew to California for a teacher conference, and my dad had a DJ-ing job. My stepbrother went to his father's, and I was actually allowed to go to my biological mom's house. I was so excited to go, to finally get to spend time with her and maybe even learn Spanish again, which I actually spoke before I spoke English.

Everything was a disaster. I got homesick and called my dad to come get me. He was so worried because I was crying that he stopped everything and came to Atlanta. Because I was not only with my biological mother, but her husband as well, my dad was freaking out. As a parent now, I totally understand the fear that can come as your child calls you crying. My step-family, however, stayed on their trips.

There is nothing specific I remember bothering me, I had never been away without my immediate family before. I was so disappointed in myself and embarrassed. How could I not be comfortable with the person who gave birth to me? To this day, I can't explain or understand that. These events allowed time with me and my dad. He reassured me no matter what happened in life, he would be there for me.

I felt the need to find a way to stand out without being an embarrassment to my family. It was assumed that what I wanted, I only wanted because of my stepbrother. Simple things like my own TV to more complex things, like eyeglasses. With the network of people my parents knew, and being the little sister of a popular kid, I couldn't embarrass the family. That's how things were in the South for black girls, and it was slowly being instilled in me. Don't embarrass the family and don't speak unless spoken to. When I told my family that I was a lesbian and that I already told my classmates, it changed everything.

I was too young to know what I wanted and I had never even had sex, so how could I know? How could I embarrass my family telling the school I was a lesbian? How did that look for my parents? What if they lost their jobs because of what I said? I couldn't answer those questions. What I did know, is everything I liked about any of the guys in school, I only liked it because I wanted to be them, not because I wanted to date them. I knew what I liked, women. It was that simple to me.

Growing into who you are can cause many disagreements with your parents. Mostly because they are trying to protect you, to keep you from making the same mistakes they made. My parents grew up during the time of Integration, so this was the only thing they knew how to compare my orientation to. They would say how I should keep it to myself and no one has to know. Adding, that when you're black you have enough problems and that's something you can't hide about yourself.

As I got older, my dad told me about my other siblings. I had an older brother who was in prison, who I knew about. Now, I also had a younger sister and a younger brother. The tension in the house began to make sense. I was angry with my dad for having more kids. I thought that he wasn't home as much because of them. My parents began to communicate less. With the lack of communication between my parents and my stepbrother being in college, I was turning into the glue trying to keep my parents together.

As long as I didn't talk about being a lesbian, my stepmother would be supportive of me as I did things in school. My father would bring up the topic in a way to keep me from wanting to be a lesbian. He would say, "How are you going to give me grandkids?" or "You want to lay with another woman? That's not going to do anything for you." It was discouraging, not in a sense of not identifying as a lesbian, but in a sense of not being "out." Unfortunately, you can't go back in the closet when it's convenient.

There were times when my stepmother and I were closer than my dad and I, and vice versa. The one event that changed my life and relationship with my father forever was right after my senior prom. A small group of students bet another student that he couldn't get this girl to go to the prom with him.

We didn't have money, and he enjoyed Black and Mild cigars, so that was the wager. I had a bag packed with a change of clothes for after the prom, and I had the cigars in that bag. I've never been a smoker, no one in our house was, to my knowledge, so that was never a habit I picked up.

As I was preparing for the prom, my stepmom went through my bag to get something and noticed the cigars. We were around her coworkers, and staying in tune with the idea of not being embarrassed, she didn't say anything out loud. She let me know she saw them and eventually told my dad.

The next day after the prom, I was sitting at the computer in the kitchen. This wasn't the time of laptops and smartphones. This was one family computer, with old school dial-up internet, so everyone knew when you were on the computer. We kept our ironing board in the kitchen as well, and my stepmother was ironing and on the phone. My father was sitting on the barstool at the counter, which was behind me.

Out of nowhere, my father asked me if I thought he was stupid? I said no. I'm sure with sarcasm and attitude that was, at this point, ingrained in me from my environment.

The room was quiet, except for my stepmom on the phone, and then a lighter flew past my face, hit the computer screen, and broke. I knew my dad was pissed off, but I didn't know how pissed he was. As I turned around to see what was going on I was met with a slap to my face. "You really think I'm stupid? You're smoking dope?!"

I was in a bit of shock, but the words made me give out a nervous laugh. I had never been near 'dope,' which I knew he was specifically speaking of marijuana. "Eww, no dad, I don't smoke," was all I could let out before being met with another blow, this time to the stomach. I remember hearing my stepmother saying to whoever was on the phone, "I'll call you back later," followed by, "Ok, that's enough." My father, who was my role model, my blood, was now a monster that I had never met.

The first thing that flashed in my mind was the trip we took to DC. I remember being young, and an older drunk man saying something to me. My dad sent the family to the hotel room, and when he returned he was sweaty, out of breath, and had his keys in his fist, like a weapon. "You don't have to worry about that guy anymore." What for so long was a heroic moment, turned into a disgusting memory. As I stood there getting hit, then laying balled up on the floor with my head covered getting kicked, I wondered if he killed that man. I wondered if I was going to die. "You want to be a man, get up, and fight me like one!" he said over and over.

I had never said I wanted to be a man at this point in my life. I knew this wasn't about the cigars. I knew I couldn't fight my father. I also knew I had to get up. So I did. I got up, grabbed some clothes, and got my bike to ride away. He snatched my bike from under me, "I paid for this, you can't have it." So, I walked. I had no idea where I was going, but I walked.

We grew up on the opposite side of town from where we went to school. I didn't know the kids in my neighborhood, only my dad's friends. One of his friends had a house with a lot of land so this was the only place I knew to hide. I sat there for what felt like hours before someone finally saw me.

My dad's best friend's nephew saw me, and he took me to his mom's house. She called my house, which I knew would make it worse, but she asked to speak to my stepmother. At this moment I learned about women's code and intuition. She told my stepmom where I was and asked where I needed to be. I stayed away from home for several weeks. The people my father grew up with knew this side of him, this fact made the situation even scarier. Things were never the same with my father after that.

The way I looked up to my father changed. I didn't know what to expect from him anymore, what would trigger this type of response again. I was angry and scared at the same time. When I returned home my father never apologized for his actions. Instead, he tried to explain why it happened. Over the years he would bring this up and give a different explanation as to why it happened. He wanted to show me that he paid for my bike and other items, not my mom, or he was worried about me buying tobacco for someone under 18 years old. Many excuses, including denying this event ever happened, but never an apology for actually putting his hands on me.

An interesting paradigm in the south is religion. I grew up going to an Episcopal church. Unlike most southern black families who went to church two or three days a week for hours at a time, we went to church every other Sunday. Our church was in Spartanburg, which is about an hour and forty-five minutes from Columbia. Since my grandmother still lived in Spartanburg, this was still the home church for my stepmother. My grandmother didn't drive, so every other weekend we would take her grocery shopping and go to church. The service was about 45 minutes and very ritualistic.

The Episcopal Church uses The Book of Common Prayer for services. We would have readings from the Bible printed out for us, but we didn't physically use the Bible often. My stepbrother and I served on the altar. We learned the order of service, helped with carrying the candles, the Cross, and even with Holy Communion sometimes. There is always Communion in the Episcopal service, to cleanse you of your last week's sins. The only exception is if there isn't someone with the proper training to administer Communion. It was made clear to me that no matter the sin, you are forgiven, as long as you believe in Christ. I accepted this as fact at a young age, only having a brief time period of religious doubt, regarding my sexuality and identity. My belief in Christ was, and still is, stronger than my doubt.

Many of the people I knew in my church were accepting of the gay community. Hearing stories of someone being kicked out or disowned for their identity was rare. It was more like, 'we all know how that child is, no need of making a fuss about it.' In college, I went to church more, and not only Episcopal services, but I also sang in the gospel choir. I once had a classmate ask me, "Why go to church? You're a lesbian, you're going to hell anyway." My foundation in Christ didn't let this comment bother me.

I stopped believing in the conventional aspects of religion, that God was a man, and that you had to go to church to be a believer. The Golden Rule was my way of life, to treat others as you want to be treated. I stopped listening to others when they said I was going to hell. Someone told my stepmother we were all going to hell simply because we were Episcopalians! I had gotten so used to being told I was going to hell, I wasn't intimidated by it anymore. As I began my transition, I had relatives ask, "Have you talked to God?" I answered, "Yes, She said I was good." This became my go-to phrase.

I have found that some religious people don't think you can believe in God AND be a part of the LGBTQ+ community. Then, to say God is She, that was a slap in the face to so many who have this colonial image of a white male Jesus. An image I believe makes no sense especially considering the region where Jesus was born. An image that, if altered, causes so much outrage instead of compassion and understanding for others wanting to see Christ like themselves.

As children, we know early who we are. We may not have the words for it, however, we are happy with who we are until others start bringing in doubt. From a very young age, I knew I would be a leader. How does this manifest in childhood? I ran for student council, became a peer mediator, and got involved in anything that was helpful to others.

In my junior year in high school, I ran for student body vice president. When I had to give my speech, I decided to wear a suit. I couldn't wear a suit and tie like I wanted, so I had on a powerful purple skirt suit. It would be a rare occasion to see me dressed in feminine clothing. When I stood up to give my speech, I got a standing ovation before I could even say my name. It was an amazing feeling! I remember looking at the teacher who was in charge of the student council and asking did I still have to give a speech? I won that election. I ran again and won the election the following year as class president.

I was the highest-ranking non-commissioned officer in our JROTC program, and I had the school record for pull-ups for a female cadet. I still held the record until about 2010. I haven't checked it in a while to see if it's still there. Although I wanted to go directly into the military as a military police officer, my stepmother, the educator, said I needed to go to college first.

2

PRESIDENTIAL STATUS

So, I applied to and got accepted into The Citadel, The Military College of South Carolina. That experience is a book all in itself! I was a member of the Regimental Band, playing the french horn, and had no idea what I had gotten myself into. I learned the ways of The Citadel, how to shine my brass, polish my shoes, do as I'm told, when I'm told, as quickly as possible. Very much like how I grew up.

I joined the African American society and the gospel choir. These two social organizations, as well as mandatory band events, kept me busy. The days felt long, but the weeks, months, and years flew by. As the 22nd black female to graduate, during the time of Don't Ask Don't Tell, going into the military wasn't an option for me personally. I had been out of the closet as a lesbian since middle school and I was not going back.

I decided to start my career in law enforcement. As a police officer, I was told I wouldn't be a cop long, because I was too nice. This concept made no sense to me, I was still a young officer with less than a year in and I'm sure a bit naive, but surely there weren't that many mean cops. I used my life experiences, all twenty-three years of it, to keep me focused on making things better for people.

As a masculine lesbian, I would often be called, "sir," "Mr.," or "man," and it didn't bother me. There actually became a point where my stepmother even called me her "Citadel man." She would say, "Come here my Citadel man and open this jar for me." This gave me a sense of pride in my personal strength. I've always had great upper body strength, so I loved my arms, my pecs, and even my upper back. I started to hate my hips, my breast, even the sound of my voice. I had imagined being a man several times in my life, how it would be to be a husband and a father. This was becoming a daily thought.

I knew I had to do something, I had to figure out a way to be the man I knew I was. I used to think you had to go overseas or to California to change your gender. I thought it was a thing on the Jerry Springer show. I had no idea I could not only stay in the United States but stay home, here in South Carolina and get the help I needed.

I began meeting other men who had transitioned, mostly online, getting their stories and advice on where to start. Some of these men were in my fraternity, which I joined in 2004. It was 2010, and I knew this was the path I needed to take to fully become me. I was able to find a doctor in North Carolina who would help me to start Hormone Replacement Therapy (HRT). I found a psychologist who referred me to a psychiatrist who, at the time, diagnosed me with Gender

Identity Disorder. This, by the way, is no longer an actual diagnosis. Best of all, I was able to find one of the best doctors for my chest reconstruction surgery (top surgery).

My scattered life of puzzle pieces was now put back together. I was a man, THE man, and I was finally happy. My name was changed, my birth certificate was changed, I am He/Him/His! The identity I knew all my life finally had a title - transgender. I was officially a transgender man named Marion Gregory Green. Now I had to figure out how to act like a man?

How do I stay true to my own ethics, morals, and personal experience while not falling into a misogynistic pattern? How do I blend when necessary, but still stand out as the leader I know I am? I would have to learn more about myself to truly answer these questions. Life's experiences would mold and shape who I became.

My core felt complete, with the proverbial inside matching the outside. With a solid foundation, it was time for Greg to have the audacity to be Greg, unapologetically. I began to learn not only how to be a man, but how to be me. I already had a great personality, enjoyed making people laugh, helping people, and spreading positivity. Now I get to do these things with others seeing me the way I saw myself.

One of my favorite movies growing up was Spike Lee's School Daze. I loved the overall message, but even more the insider view on what it meant to be in a sorority or fraternity. As a Citadel Cadet, there wasn't direct access to pledge into a black sorority. I didn't think I would be a good fit in a sorority anyway. I wasn't comfortable in dresses or feminine clothing and I knew pledging into a male fraternity wasn't going to happen either. Although there had been rumors of underground pledging of men into the sororities, that concept was not very popular amongst the Divine Nine (D9), and I had only seen a few underground pledging of women into male fraternities.

In the summer of 2004, I pledged into a fraternity. With my stepmother's family having several members in the D9, I was excited about joining this organization. I was hoping my stepmother would share in my excitement, however, since we weren't D9 and relatively new, she felt it was fake. "That won't last long," was her reply.

This organization was created for dominant lesbian women and our goal was to provide community service to all and to dismantle stereotypes around the LGBTQ+ community. Alpha Psi Kappa Fraternity, Inc. was founded in 2002, making me one of its earliest members. I met others who I had many things in common with and who lived all across the country. We began to travel together, doing community service all over the nation,

The first trip I went on was to Atlanta. I was still in college. I had mentioned the trip to my stepmother weeks in advance. She told me as long as my grades had improved, I'd be able to go. I worked hard, got my grades up, and paid for the trip. When it was time to go, she told me if I went to Atlanta, she wouldn't speak to me again. I thought this was extreme, so I didn't believe her. I talked to my dad about this, and he agreed that since my grades were up, I should go. He also added that I was over 18 therefore an adult, and needed to make my own decisions.

I was so excited to be going on a trip away from home! I was going to meet people I had only connected with over the internet. This was also the first trip with my girlfriend that wasn't for school. I'll tell you more about her later. On this trip, I would meet people who would become lifelong friends.

I began to take more trips with this group and do more work in the community. Volunteering at various food pantries across the country, cleaning up trash off of the highways, building homes, and helping after school kids with homework. We were making a difference in our community.

At this point, I served on the national executive board as the guard, and it was time to elect a new fraternal president. I looked through all of the eligible members for president and called them individually to see who was interested in the position. As I spoke to other members, many told me I'd be good for the position. Still looking to find that leadership role in my life, I decided to move forward with running for president and was elected.

I was amazed by how many people supported my decision. I began to develop friendships all across the country, Florida, Virginia, and California. This was an amazing time for me.

As I filled in the duties of the president, I learned more about myself. I took more trips with the fraternity, I started to feel comfortable in my skin, and developed amazing friendships. I was able to share things about my life, relationship, and goals.

One of the members of the fraternity would drive up to South Carolina from Florida almost every three months to visit in person. As our relationship grew, she told me that I had saved her life. Literally. Having been on the other end of that story, I totally understood what she meant. To know that I was able to do for someone what was done for me, made me feel good.

I knew that I was helping and not only one person, but many people. I also learned that helping others made me feel important and was gratifying. There were members of the fraternity who had begun their gender transition. This was something I had thought about for so long. To see people actually doing it was fascinating to me. At this point, I was focusing on my own identity. I spoke with these fraternity members and learned a lot about what transitioning meant.

I took some time to myself and seriously thought about who I was. I thought and prayed about what life would mean if I took this journey. Would I be able to stay in my relationship? Would I be able to keep my job? Will my family cut me off? These are all of the questions that came across my mind. The only thing I thought I knew was I'd be able to count on my fraternity family to stick with me. I had built these great relationships over the past seven years, however, I had no idea the ride I was about to go on.

I was so wrong. The one place I knew would be accepting of me told me there was no place for me. An organization designed for dominant lesbian women, could not be led by a man. That's what I heard over and over again. When I reached out to my friends, I was told it was nothing personal, only business. This safe place that I had been involved with for so long, seven of its nine-year existence, was now foreign.

I continued to take trips with the fraternity and decided to try and blend with everyone. I became the photographer. I was always at an event, never in a picture. As the distance grew between me and some of the members, a new task was at hand. The development of a fraternity for transgender men. See, what makes our organization different from others, is we are a small unit in a larger Greek family.

That family started with three organizations, and after understanding the need for transgender individuals to have a space of their own, we added two more organizations.

Since I already had experience as a fraternity president, I became the first president of the newly formed organization for transmen. This was a boost for me. I was able to show other men across the country that there was a space for us. We still had to follow the guidelines for community service, so we did some of the same events as the rest of the larger family.

We opened our space to transmen all over. Some who had never heard of non-collegiate fraternities all the way to those who had previously been in D9 sororities. Men who were doctors, nurses, writers, and activists had joined us. What a proud space to be in!

After pushing the limits to some of my friendships, and then being a part of this newly created space, I began feeling more at peace. I knew there were others who didn't understand what it meant to be transgender. This is where I started to truly realize where my life long fight would be. Because of the fraternity's national recognition, and my position as president, I was asked to speak at a pride lunch in Washington, DC. This was for the Department of Justice, as someone with law enforcement experience, I was excited about the opportunities. I began speaking at different places about what it was like to be transgender. I finally found my calling, my moment of leading that I had been training for my whole life, the fight for transgender equality.

M. GREG GREEN

3

POWER COUPLE DISMANTLED

We met at the Citadel. This was a place that historically
didn't want either of us there. They taught all cadets how to
present their best selves no matter what. For those around us,
our relationship looked flawless, however, it was highly toxic.
Early in our relationship, I asked my partner how she would
feel about me being a man? She said she wouldn't stay with
me. I didn't bring it back up. I enjoyed our relationship … for
the most part. She was the cheerleader, and I was the band
geek. It was a storybook relationship, well, at least a 1990's
TV show.

After we graduated, we bought a house and moved in
together. Initially, since I knew I wanted to work in law
enforcement, we were going to move to the DC area. I didn't
think we'd actually last after college, so I got a job a month
after graduation at home and looked for a house. She had
moved back home to Virginia and also got a job quickly after

graduation. She was not very happy when I told her I was getting a house. She drove from Virginia to help me pick things out for the house, floor and countertop colors, and paint. Once it was finished, I closed on the house, and she moved in. When you're 22-years-old, this looks like love.

Because I was the president of the fraternity, many members began to call us Barack and Michelle. It gave us a high standard to live up to. My parents had their issues, and hers did also. My dad and stepmother were at a point where they could walk past each other in the house and not speak, but they would sleep in the same bed. Her parents would speak to each other in the house and sleep in separate rooms. These examples taught us how not to be.

We decided to make a relationship deal. If either of us got to a point like either of our parents, then we would let the other know and work out what was next. We both graduated with degrees in Psychology, we thought what we were doing would build a healthy relationship.

We shared what we called our, "deal breakers," what would end our relationship no matter what. I told her domestic violence was mine, and cheating was hers. It was settled. We knew the line in the sand, wherever we were in our lives. Unfortunately, it's easier said than done. At this point, I was already in law enforcement so I had all the book knowledge and some hands-on experience dealing with domestic violence. She also had all the knowledge of keywords that would get the attention of police officers. Domestic Violence, however, is hard to recognize in your own space.

It started with small disagreements over what to me seemed simple. We had four pets, two cats and two dogs. I never had cats before, only dogs growing up, so I didn't know how to care for cats. One day, I went outside with one of the cats to talk to a neighbor. Some noise spooked the cat. She jumped out of my arms and ran off. I thought she ran back to the house, because that's what I'm used to dogs doing, they go home. So, I didn't chase her, I continued my conversation.

When I got to the house and realized she wasn't there, I looked around, and then I told my fiance that I lost the cat. While I loved the cat very much, I wasn't one to freak out about these things. I thought that my lack of emotional response was a trigger for her outrage. She yelled and screamed, even going outside of the house for the neighbors to hear. Keep in mind this was highly embarrassing to me, as someone who came from a, "don't embarrass me," household.

She came back into the house, took a large bookcase, and threw it to the ground. Books, awards, and other random house decorations fell to the floor, some even broke. I was shocked! I had no idea what to do or why that was an okay response. She was mad at me for several days. During that time, I couldn't truly express how I felt due to fear of it happening again.

This wasn't the first sign that she had anger issues. The thing that happens when you're in an abusive relationship, physically or emotionally, is you don't always notice the red flags at first. There was one point while we were in college that she got upset with me and threw a remote control close to my face. When I mentioned that it almost hit my face she said, "If I wanted to hit you, I would have."

She got mad at me once, took off her engagement ring, and threw it. I was still paying for the ring and it took hours to find it. I now realize how toxic this was. How she manipulated me time and time again by walking a fine line of physical abuse and fully engaging in mental abuse. Ironically, she reminded me a lot of my stepmother, playing mental games with me, like how my stepmother explained the types of people in Panama.

We could feel our relationship getting out of control and decided to go to counseling. We had two therapists we visited, one as a couple, and one I went to on my own. At this point in my life, I had not started my transition, many states were acknowledging same-sex marriages, but it was not legal on a federal level. We were simply a lesbian couple who had a wedding with our friends and family.

Two main issues came up while we were in therapy. One was education. She had gone on to get her master's degree and was working on her doctorate. I had no desire to go back to school, I had a hard enough time academically graduating from The Citadel. She felt that a couple that had different levels of education couldn't last and not going back to school was to help end our relationship. The other issue was children.

I always thought I was a mistake, that my biological mother had me to get my dad to marry her. My dad often said that because my mother was pregnant didn't mean he was going to marry her. So, I think that planted the seed that grew into the idea that she tried to use me to get citizenship.

Since I felt this way all of my life, I never thought about bringing children into the world. I was also a realist. I felt that we weren't in a good position to have kids as a couple, both from our relationship standpoint, and financial. We weren't like other couples, we couldn't have sex and try to have kids, we had to go buy sperm and go through a whole process.

These conversations became our daily arguments. Regardless of what started it, it ended in kids or education. She came home one day and started telling me about a transgender guy in her class. I was partially intrigued, but also a bit jealous of the depth of their conversations, so I didn't fully listen. She got the guy on the phone and passed the phone to me. I didn't know who it was and she knew I didn't like answering a phone call without knowing who is on the other end.

"Don't hang up." He started. As much as I wanted to hang up, I didn't want to be rude. "Have you ever felt that you are a man?" When he asked this, I started crying. It was not the reaction I thought I would have. I was overwhelmed with emotion.

All the years of discarding who I was, then to have someone ask such a simple question seemed to open a box I hid so deeply within myself. Of course, I felt like a man, all of my life, what was I supposed to do about it?

This man, who was once someone who made me jealous, was now in my house explaining to not only me but my then-wife, the journey of transition. He told us how it was a strain on his relationship, and once he began his journey, they were able to live happily again.

This was our boost. I personally began to understand what transitioning meant to me. She started looking up doctors, I started calling my health insurance to see what was covered. Things were going in a good direction for us.

The conversation of transitioning derailed the previous arguments of kids and education. However, because of her passion, I knew those arguments would come back. This new topic of transitioning became a project for her.

This new enlightenment was great for me, I mean, I was the beneficiary of the hard work of looking everything up. I got my name changed. We found a doctor to administer testosterone and begin my medical transition. Then we found a doctor to do my chest reconstruction surgery, also known as, top surgery. The only part of this that was available in South Carolina was the name change.

All of this happened in less than a year's time. The final and most important step was changing my gender on my birth certificate. Because the state didn't, and still doesn't, have a form or protocol for this, we had to create a form. We did and it worked. After explaining to the judge how the change would appear on my birth certificate, she was ok with signing the papers.

Legally, everything was taken care of. Her project was over, and I knew, so was our relationship. I was stressed every day by the arguments that had returned as I knew they would. I started venting to people, no one in particular, anywho who would listen. See, I already knew my hard line in the relationship was domestic violence. However, it took someone else to point out the verbal abuse.

The random tantrums of tearing up the house was a form of domestic violence. This "someone else," also wanted to be with me. I can't say that I was innocent in the breaking up of our relationship. I tested the line several times in regards to cheating until I tested that line too far.

I was ashamed of myself and I didn't know how to tell her what I did. So, like some cheaters, I didn't say anything. I did, however, fight through my fear and tell her our relationship was over. As much as I thought about trying to make it work, it didn't make sense to push through something I didn't think was worth it. After all, we had been through, I knew she would feel the same way. First came the tantrum, she smashed everything in the house. Literally, she threw bookcases and chairs, anything she could touch.

I knew she was upset, but now I was worried about my safety. Not because of her, but there was a new reality in my life. I am a black man, in a trashed house, with a woman who was at this point, bleeding from cutting herself on something. A woman who knew everything that needed to be said to police officers to get me arrested.

I was no longer employed by my police agency. However, I was still looking for jobs in that field. I grabbed my phone to call on a few friends of ours to come over and help. They were able to help us calm down and decided we needed to go to the hospital because we thought she broke her arm.

While this was going on, I decided I had to leave. I couldn't live like this and I didn't need this to be my everyday life. I grabbed a few things, got in my car, and left. My wife was from Virginia, so she didn't have as many people here as I did. I called her mom and suggested her parents come and get her. It was near the holidays so this seemed to be a good idea.

I ended up living in my car for about a month and a half. I would go to my house when she wasn't home to get things and shower, then go park somewhere. This was usually a hospital parking lot where I wouldn't stand out. One day I went home, and the lock had been changed. I never got an automatic garage door opener, so I went in through the garage, got all my legal documents and more of my personal items, and loaded everything I could into my car. I was so glad I had a 1989 Oldsmobile Delta 88! There was so much room in there, so I was able to save a lot of items.

I was working in a restaurant at this point. When I got to work someone said to me, "There's a police officer looking for you." I thought it was one of my old shift buddies, so I was excited to go see them. Turns out it was a server, you know, the kind that gives you a stack of papers and says, "You've been served." I was so embarrassed. I looked at them and she was actually serving me with divorce papers.

I called my Godfather, an attorney, and asked what I was supposed to do with this. He told me nothing. I was irritated by his response at first, but then he explained. If the state of South Carolina makes you stay separated for a year, then actually go through a divorce, that means they recognized your same-sex marriage. This was now bigger than me, so I stepped back and let the time go by.

4

10-7

Being a police officer is something I have always wanted to do. I saw it as a way to give back while being as masculine as I wanted without much issue. Initially, I wanted to be an MP, military police, in the army. However, as I mentioned before, Don't Ask Don't Tell, was in effect during what would have been my prime time to join. While at The Citadel, I started the process of joining the Police Corps, a program that would pay for college and give me a job right out of school. This was similar to military programs. Due to a decrease in government funding, the Police Corps program was shut down before I graduated.

One of my stepmother's coworkers suggested I get a job on the force where I grew up. One thing that made this agency stand out was the fact that it was both Police and Fire, which would be great on my resume, as I had plans to go into federal law enforcement. I applied, interviewed, and got the job. I was excited about the possibilities of my career.

The first part of my training was the police academy. As they prepared our class, we were split into separate squads. They asked those who want to be leaders within the group to step forward. From what you've read about me so far, you probably think I stepped up. Well, I didn't.

In South Carolina, you don't have to be a college graduate to be in law enforcement. As a Citadel graduate, I spent four years fine-tuning my leadership skills. I didn't see what nine weeks at the academy was going to do to make a major impression on my ability to lead, so I afforded the opportunity to someone else.

In fact, it wasn't until the final weeks of the academy that one of the trainers approached me about not being the class leader. When I explained my logic to him, he assured me this decision was a sign of true leadership. It was reassuring to have someone who retired from the military and highway patrol to think so highly of me.

After graduating from the police academy and a few weeks of in-house training, I was out on my own. I had my own patrol car and took great pride in my career. I knew it was my job to protect and serve. I also knew there weren't many black officers in the department, so I felt an extra duty to be seen by the citizens of the city.

One of the police officers was so happy to have a black female on the team, he immediately wanted me to work as an undercover officer. This was not something I wanted to do. I also knew this would not work since I knew so many people in the area. Not only was this the city I grew up in but the city where both of my parents worked.

If someone didn't know me from school, they knew me because of my parents. He took a chance anyway taking me on a drug call and I was immediately recognized. The only good thing is the person didn't know I was a cop. This moment proved that undercover work wasn't for me.

So, I fully invested in the idea of community policing. I walked around the various schools, neighborhoods, and shopping centers so people would be more comfortable when seeing police officers. The idea that because you see a cop doesn't mean something bad is happening, is one I wanted to portray.

I began to know the people of the city. I learned more about my classmates and their family dynamics. Once I was flagged down by this lady while I was driving. She drove past me, turned around, and started flashing her headlights. So I stopped, positioned myself not to be a target, and approached her vehicle. She was the mother of a young man I went to both high school and The Citadel with. She was crying and I didn't know what was wrong. "He has uncles that have gone to The Citadel and he was never interested until you went. I want you to know he's a police officer now too, and you've had such a positive influence over his life choices." I was shocked! I didn't realize this kid, a freshman when I was a senior, twice, was even paying me any attention. It was a good feeling to know I helped someone move in a positive direction in their life.

Many police officers have certain laws that are their main focus. Some officers focus on speeding tickets, others, narcotics. My focus had become seatbelt tickets, underage drinking, and DUI (Driving Under the Influence). To me it was simple, I had lost too many classmates to DUI's, several who weren't old enough to drink, and some who weren't wearing seatbelts. I had participated in training to learn standardized sobriety tests, which are used all across the nation. My prosecution rate was high. Meaning, those I stopped, plead or were found guilty. I even got an award from the South Carolina Highway Patrol for the amount of DUI prosecutions I had in a year.

I felt like my career was going well. I continued to take special training and participate in various topics from Domestic Violence to Gangs. When my personal and professional life crossed paths, the moment I decided to begin my transition from female to male, I had no idea how to tell my job. On one hand, it was health-related and should have been protected under health privacy laws. On the other hand, at some point, my changes would become obvious and would surely be addressed.

I decided to tell my shift, the team I worked with on a regular, that I would be changing my gender. I had no idea what it would mean as work continued, but I wanted them to know. I told them on the same night I took my first shot of Testosterone. I didn't know what changes would happen or how soon they would happen, because each person's body responds differently. My team seemed to be okay with it. "You're one of the guys anyway," one of them said.

Well, that was that. The hard part of coming out again was done. It was back to work as usual, or so I thought. I started noticing little things, like conversations stopping when I came into a room. People who used to speak started distancing themselves from me. I knew I was in a conservative department, even the Chief had confederate flag pictures in his office. I also knew it was time to start looking for another job. I thought it would have been easier to go to another department and make as smooth of a career transition as possible, so I started applying.

In the meantime, I continued working as well as transitioning. I had turned in my FMLA papers for my surgery date. Other than the conversations stopping, and people distancing themselves from me, nothing major had changed. Nothing I could pinpoint.

One night I volunteered to work a shift opposite of mine because they were short-staffed. This shift changed my life. Based on a vehicle description provided by another officer, I made a traffic stop that night. After making contact with the driver, I placed her under arrest for DUI. During my sobriety test, another officer actually arrested one of the passengers, for what, I wasn't sure of at the time.

Back in 2011, the way the law worked was like this; if someone provided a breath sample blood alcohol content (BAC) of .05 or higher, it was presumed they were under the influence of alcohol. If their BAC was .04 or lower, the officer could request a urine sample to test for drugs. One of the things that made me good at DUI prosecutions is that I understood DUI didn't mean under the influence of alcohol, it also meant any drug, street or prescription, that was going to impair your driving. Another SC law was once you arrested someone for DUI, even after the testing, you couldn't release them, only a judge could do that.

Once everything was said and done, I stood by my decision to arrest the driver. I knew there was something going on in her system that was keeping her from driving properly. Several weeks went by and it was about time for me to prepare to leave for my top surgery. I got called into the lieutenant's office and told I should not have made that arrest. I had neither probable cause nor jurisdiction to do so.

After some back and forth, I was written up and given a one-day suspension. I knew this was coming, I didn't think that would be the call that did it, but I knew something was coming. It was strange because I was asked to pick the day off I wanted. "This isn't a vacation," I continued, "this is punishment, you tell me the date not to come in."

Things went downhill after that. I kept my head low and my applications to other jobs flowing. Then it was time for my surgery, so I had about eight weeks to get away from everyone. During my healing, I found out that I had been demoted.

Upon my return to work, I was told, along with the written reprimand and one-day suspension that I already had, I was going to be on probation. I didn't understand how I could still be getting punished for something that happened four months ago.

I knew there was nothing to understand, this was going to be their way to get me out of the department. I had not heard anything back from the other departments I applied to. The two things that were keeping me going was my second job at a restaurant and the fact that I was starting to look and feel more like the man I've always been. I got my legal documents changed to reflect my name and gender. Since I was told I was a liability at work, I thought this would be perfect to change. I turned in my new birth certificate, so no longer was I "mid-transition," for all legal purposes, my transition was complete. The liability was gone, I was all-male now.

Two weeks later, I was fired. Only, it wasn't a firing. It was the end of my career. I applied to several agencies, local municipalities, counties, and state-level departments. I got a few no's, but mostly I received no callbacks. Nothing. Silence.

No one wanted to hire me, and no one wanted to say why they wouldn't hire me.

For years, I continued to apply for jobs in law enforcement. My certification would only stay good for two years. Letting go of this career was hard for me. I didn't expect it to end without my consent. So many officers I had seen get in fights and make other poor decisions, were still wearing the badge. Mine was gone. I was forever 10-7, out of service. I lost my purpose. All I wanted to do was help people and this was the only way I knew how.

5

SPIRAL OF 2012

Since my transition began, I lost connection with many of my fraternity friends. I had already lost my job and I knew I couldn't stay in my current relationship. By December, everything seemed to implode and I was all alone when 2012 started. During this time I was living in my car. I was still working in a restaurant so I had that, but the only thing I thought to pay when it came to bills was my car insurance and gas.

I still lived close to my parents and my childhood home, but I was too anxious to go back there. Once I moved out, going back never seemed like an option. I didn't have to hide who I was in my own space nor did I have to pretend to be someone else. I knew how my parents reacted to the idea of me being a lesbian, I could only imagine how worse it would be if I told them everything I was going through while transitioning.

I started hanging out with some folks from the restaurant. They were so glad I wasn't a cop anymore because they could relax around me. In other words, they didn't have to hide their drug habits. At first, I cared, but after a while, I didn't. I worked hard, and I played even harder. I began to binge drink. I would go to the bar with my friends, and wouldn't leave until the sun came up. I've always been a drinker, however, this was a new level for me. I didn't care about much and neither did those around me, we were often each other's cheerleaders to drink more.

Bartenders at several places would serve me my first drink as soon as I walked in, they already knew what I was having and that I would be good on my tab. They knew my name, and my club name, which I still use to this day.

Not soon after, I visited a high school friend, to catch up and tell her what was going on in my life. Her mom was apparently listening to the conversation and said, "If you want to, you can stay here." I told her thank you but didn't make much more of it. I knew her daughter was in school out of state, so there was a room open, but I didn't want to be a burden to anyone.

I continued waiting tables during the day and drinking at night. Since I was sleeping in my car, I slept at the bar if I couldn't drive to a hospital to sleep. The problem came when I stopped being able to realize I shouldn't be driving. As I mentioned before, DUI arrests were important to me because I lost too many friends to drunk drivers. There was a part of me that knew I was going down the wrong path, I simply didn't know how to get myself under control.

Sleeping in the car started to get cold. If you recall, I mentioned I was in an older car, so it took a lot of gas, especially to run for heat. A coworker from the restaurant knew I was sleeping in the car and she told me I needed to stay with my friend's mom. I messaged her and asked if this was still ok? She said sure.

I had been living on my own for about five years. Yes, my parents still lived in the area, but I was too ashamed to tell them what I was going through. I didn't even tell them I had been served with divorce papers. I knew I would get ridiculed for "letting" someone else take my house and losing my job. I knew it would all be blamed on transitioning.

See, when I started transitioning I had no idea how I was going to tell my parents. They were both already not speaking to each other, so to get them in the same place was going to be hard. Ironically, I got into an accident in my patrol car, and I figured this was the time to get them together. As it turns out, my stepmother was out of town, and my dad showed up with one of his lady friends. So as you can see that didn't go as planned. I did go ahead and tell my dad about me transitioning and he wasn't happy.

For the first time in my life, I reached for a hug and he didn't hug me back. That hurt my feelings, however, I had prepared myself as much as possible for this outcome. My therapist helped me prepare for the fact that I might lose everyone who wasn't ready for me to be me. I did eventually tell my stepmother about my transition, she was unhappy as well and in her normal snarky way said, "Cutting off your tits isn't going to make you happy." It wasn't about the surgery for me. It was about the world seeing me as I saw myself.

Here I am, now living under someone else's roof. While she worked in the school system, she wasn't a teacher, she was a counselor and strong in her religious beliefs. I was prepared to be misgendered and pressured into going to her church. The idea of reliving personal trauma made me very anxious, which then added to my drinking. I had no reason to feel this way, I was only creating scenarios in my head and allowing my anxiety to take control.

Turned out I had nothing to worry about! Ms. Courtenay always respected me. We could have religious conversations without judgment. She never asked for a dime for rent or anything. I tried to leave money around, and she'd give it back to me saying, "I think you dropped this." So, I started buying groceries, trying to do yard work, as best I could, (my allergies are terrible), and making sure the house was good.

I was still working hard at the restaurant and drinking as hard when I was off. I knew Ms. Courtenay had to get up early for work, and although she gave me a key and no curfew, I still wouldn't come home if it was after midnight. She wasn't much of a drinker either, so I didn't have much when I was in the house. I would make her simple mixed drinks on the weekends. We would sit on the porch and talk and drink margaritas. I didn't hide the fact that I drank, only how much.

One evening I was headed home after bar hopping and I knew I should not have been driving. Everything in me was saying stop, pull over, get there later. I had no rush to get to the house, I was making a poor decision. So many times you hear people say they fell asleep at the wheel, well, that's what alcohol will do to you. It's not only something that happens because people are tired.

There's a church on the corner of the street that I turn down to get to Ms. Courtenay's. As I'm getting closer to her house, I try my best to stay focused to get there. Knowing I had no business behind the wheel, I actually started crying and praying. I was so mad at myself, but still wouldn't pullover. I knew that if I pulled over, and the car was still running, I could still get charged with a DUI per the state law. So, since I was so close, I kept going. I heard and felt a loud bump and woke up. I fell asleep. No, I passed out. When I regained consciousness, I realized I had driven my car across three lanes over the curb, perfectly between two trees, and stopped right in the middle of the churchyard.

I had never been more disappointed in myself. I had lost the last four hours of my life, I had no idea how long I had been there. No idea what or who else I may have hurt, scared, or come close to hurting. I knew better than this. This was totally unacceptable. Landing in the church was clearly a sign from the Divine. It was time for a change.

I decided to stop drinking. I didn't want to work on controlling how much I drink, I wanted to stop. I knew if I couldn't stop, then I would have to get professional help. I didn't think I was at that point - yet. I spoke to Ms. Courtenay about what I was going through. She was a counselor so why not get some advice.

I was able to control my life. I went to work all the time. I stopped going to the bars and left any alcohol I had in the trunk of my car. I decided I needed to do something better with my life and really get back to being my best self.

I was so thankful to my coworker for pushing me to go to Ms. Courtenay's. She had become a part of my life as I was navigating all of these changes. We had actually started working at the restaurant at the same time. Her cousin, who's father had a police substation named after him, got us both the job.

I began to hang around their family more. I enjoyed watching how they celebrated everyone, Easter, birthdays, and anniversaries. They had a large family, that was so diverse and everyone seemed to get along. It made me think of my family. Maybe one day this would be something we could achieve.

6

BECOMING A FATHER

I mentioned a few chapters back that one of the arguments my ex used to have with me was about wanting children. That argument was an ebb and flow of me not wanting kids until I realized I wasn't against it. I was terrified of the idea of raising a child alone, but having someone helping me wasn't as scary. I also realized that many parents don't know what to do, especially with their first child, so why not? To her, it was as if I was only saying that to end the conversation. When I finally got to truly thinking about having kids, that's how she would shut me down. It made me feel like she was trying to confuse me. My coworker had three kids and it was cool to interact with them.

I never had a chance to interact with kids, so I didn't know what it would be like to even consider being a parent. Her kids were about six years old, four years old, and about three months. The youngest child became one of the smallest children I've ever held. Not that he was that tiny, it was because I didn't hold babies. I guess I experienced what they call, "baby fever," at that moment.

As our friendship grew into something more, my coworker and I decided to have a serious conversation. We knew we wanted more from each other, but we also knew I was barely out of a long relationship. So, we had to be careful and aware of false feelings. In other words, the rebound effect.

We started riding to work together, our schedules were similar so this made sense. She lived with her mom and I was still at Ms. Courtenay's, but we were only five minutes away. Her place became a safe space for me. I could help around the house and I felt needed.

Although I already had my degree, I was having problems getting a job. It was determined I was overqualified for most of the jobs I put in for. My coworker convinced me to go to the local technical school and get a two-year degree to go along with my bachelor's degree. This wasn't a bad idea, especially since I had student loans. As long as I was in school, I didn't have to pay on my loans. It's not the best way to get rid of a bill, but it's something I had to do to keep some of my finances under control.

I decided to go back to school for business administration. I never was a fan of school, but this would be the first time I'd be in school as a man. School was a bit different than I was used to, a little because of my age and a lot because of not being a military school. I felt like the old dude in class. As I started to pull out my notebooks and pencils, the other students pulled out laptops. I thought I was already going to be behind in work at this rate. What I was learning in school was helpful not only to the ideas of me moving up within the restaurant but also in my own life. The financial classes were helping me get my personal finances back on track. I was also learning more about corporate world examples that I was able to mix with the previous military examples given at The Citadel.

While I wasn't getting the jobs I wanted, I thought that if I learned more about business I would be able to make some progress at the restaurant. I learned the ins and outs of the restaurant while I was working, dishwashing, bartending, hosting, waiting tables, and even working on the grill. I decided I wanted to go into management with the hopes of having my own building one day.

As my relationship with my coworker grew, so did my relationship with her youngest child. He was the cutest baby I had seen. As he began learning to speak, he started calling me Dada. This scared me! I didn't want to confuse this kid, but I had not seen his dad around.

This prompted a conversation about his biological father and what my role was going to be. I made it clear that I didn't want this child to go through the same things I went through. As long as his father was not abusive, I wanted to be sure he was in his life. In the meantime, I was there.

I took this kid in as my own, as much as a guy who didn't have his own place could. My coworker, now girlfriend, pushed for me to get back into my house. This wasn't going to be an easy task, especially emotionally. My ex was still in the house, and the divorce papers came with a restraining order. I wasn't supposed to go anywhere near my own home. I found out what I needed to do to evict her and the fact that she wasn't paying the mortgage made it a bit easier to get her out.

Once I was back in my home, I asked my new girlfriend to come live with me. As I was taking the role of father for this young child, my first thought was to provide a safe home for my family. I knew that meant her, her baby boy, and even possibly the older two children would be in my home. At the time, the older two were living with their father. It was what was best for everyone as she was preparing to move out of her mother's house.

One summer she asked if the kids could come to visit. I said of course and added that they could stay if that's what she wanted. I could never see myself telling a mother her children couldn't live with her. My only stipulation was that we would all be involved with the kids. I understood there would be certain things I couldn't do for the older two, but I wanted them to also know I would be there to support them in school and whenever they needed.

Our relationship was working out well. We both agreed it was a relationship built out of convenience, me wanting to have someone to be with and help me with my home, and her having her own place to stay with her kids.

Her baby boy became my baby boy. His father, although we never blocked him, seemed to not want to be involved. I took care of this young man. We went to the doctor for all his shots, found a dentist for him, and put him in the best daycare. I gave him his first hair cut, helped him with his first steps, and taught him to ride a bike. I did my best not to make him feel any different than his older siblings, who saw their father often. I picked up a second job so I was working two jobs and going to school, then coming home and doing the family thing. It was a lot and it was beautiful all at the same time.

7

FRESH START

The restaurant was my main job. I had picked up several different jobs as my second job and left them if it didn't work out with my schedule. I would give everything I had to make the jobs work, but trying to balance everything was difficult. I knew I needed to focus on one task. I applied to a shipping company at the airport and got the job.

This was the fresh start I needed. A new man, a new job, new coworkers, and learning new skills. As much as I enjoy making friends, I tried hard to focus on the job. I was taught to show up early, leave late, and make an impression. That's what I did. When there were extra work hours, I was there. I went to other locations to help with moving packages and loading up trucks.

One burden that came with this fresh start was being closeted again. I didn't talk about my past life or my transition. It's not that I was ashamed of who I was, I didn't want to lose this new opportunity. Although this company was worldwide, and had several non-discrimination policies, I knew the actual work environment could be toxic, and I didn't want to push any buttons.

This concept was difficult for me, I had been out as a member of the LGBTQ+ community since I was about 11 or 12 years old. I never worried about how others saw me or how others would treat me until now. I had already lost my career in law enforcement, I wasn't ready to go through anything like that again, especially on the basis of simply being myself.

After losing my policing career and not having a plan B, my finances were in turmoil. I had no idea how I was going to keep my house, which was now in foreclosure, and pay all my bills. That's why I worked so hard. As much as I wanted this shipping company to be my only job, I knew it wasn't going to be enough to get me back to even financially. I picked up more small jobs, at one point having three at once.

I worked hard and came home still trying to provide for my new family. Regardless of anyone's family dynamic, it takes a strong house to have someone working three jobs at once. My girlfriend was working too. She had left the restaurant and found a warehouse job. The workload and the family balance were heavy for both of us. This was the first time I had to take care of so many people.

I still made sure all parents had an equal stake in what was happening with the kids. I refused to let anyone be left out of their lives who wanted to be there. I had learned so much about myself and my mothers, that I couldn't see letting that type of relationship happen again knowingly.

Since there was always negativity when speaking of my biological mother when I was growing up, I wanted to create a relationship with her as I got older. I wrote her letters when I was in college and when I got out. I connected with her and I was in a good place mentally when it came to her. I was able to visit her and speak to her a few months before she passed away. I knew she was sick and had been through a lot medically, so it was as if she wanted to see me before she passed on. When it came to the kids who now lived with me, I didn't want them to have similar stories of missing out or gaps of time in their lives when it came to their parents.

On the other side of the parental situation, is not allowing toxic parents to speak negatively to or about the kids. My son's father was negative energy. Everyone matures at different times, and it seemed to me that he still had issues with my girlfriend and allowed that to cloud his judgment as a parent. I didn't know his story, or what his thoughts were on being a parent. I only knew how he would yell, fuss, and curse about things. I didn't like this negativity around my son. My son was young and happy. I wanted him to stay this way as long as possible.

My son became my motivation for everything. I worked hard to provide for him. I did what I thought parents should do. I also wanted him to have a relationship with as much family as possible because family is important. So one day, I took him to meet my dad. My dad, although still young at heart, lit up when he saw him. His first concern, which I understand more now, was my involvement with a "ready-made" family. We had a long conversation about being careful and how things would be different for me now as a black man.

This was an early acceptance conversation that meant a lot to me. To be sitting with my dad, getting advice on how to be a dad with no judgment or negativity about my transition, was a wonderful feeling. The only condition my dad had was he didn't want to be called grandpa or grand anything. So it was decided, my son would call my father "G-pop."

Since I was working on getting my life back on track, I also reached out to my stepmother. I decided to take my son to meet her on Mother's Day. I had seen my dad light up when they met, and I had seen my stepmom light up when she met young children. As a retired educator and a stepparent herself, I thought this would be a great Mother's Day surprise.

I was wrong. As I sat and forced myself to have a conversation with my stepmother, I watched her literally ignore a two-year-old. Growing up, I had already experienced her "ignore ability" first hand. I aired on the side of caution, thinking that maybe she had the same concerns my father did. So I talked about my previous conversation with him a bit. How I was being careful and realized that ultimately I had no legal say in my son's life. But that shouldn't stop me from being a good parent for him, like her being my stepmother didn't stop her from being a good parent. She wasn't hearing it. She said I was stupid and shouldn't be worrying about anyone's child. She then went into how me being transgender was only going to confuse my son and I didn't need to deal with any children - ever.

Needless to say, that was the end of that conversation. I picked up my kid and left. I know I didn't have all the answers, but neither did she. If she did, our own relationship wouldn't be so straining.

I was further motivated to get my life together after meeting with my stepmother. I knew I had to prove her wrong about everything. I worked harder at the shipping company and got promoted. Although it was still part-time, the pay increase was now the same as I was making before leaving the police department.

I started to learn more about what the process was to become a trainer. My manager at the time said I didn't want to be a trainer and therefore he wouldn't send me to get certified. I could feel myself hitting that wall again. The wall of doubt and uncertainty. I was doubting myself and everything that was being said to me at work was validated by my own fears. I worried if I fought too much to move up, someone would "out" me or dig more into why I wasn't in law enforcement, so I stopped trying to progress. I let my fears allow someone else to tell me what path to choose in my own career.

When I stopped pushing forward, I started to notice a lack of progress with my girlfriend. I thought if I was going to be working all the time, she should too. After all, she had three kids to provide for. I started becoming resentful for the work I was doing like I was working harder than all the biological parents. Although it was my choice, I didn't want to be the only one pushing for success. It was immature of me to think my way to success would be like everyone else's, but that's where I was.

I let this toxic way of thinking take over me. Our relationship started failing and I didn't know how to save it. I didn't even know if I wanted to save it. I mostly wanted to stay friends and stay a father. Regardless, I knew things weren't working out. She knew it too. We got to a point where conversations turned into arguments and neither of us was happy.

We didn't stay at this stage long. She gathered her things and said she was leaving. I remembered feeling numb. I thought I was going to break up with her. I wasn't mad that we were over, we both knew it wasn't working, maybe I was mad because I didn't make the cut-off. It wasn't so much that, as it was my fear of never seeing my son again. The stories my father told me of how things went with my older brother's mom and him, were sitting in my head. I didn't want my son to think I abandoned him.

I also knew that this child was young. He may or may not remember me if I am totally out of the picture. When you've imagined a future for a child, and then you have no idea if you'll ever see that future, it is a tough feeling.

I had been on testosterone for several years now and I found crying difficult. This situation made me cry. The idea of losing someone I was ready to build my life around, made me cry, but it was more than that. If I were to ever be fully involved in bringing a child into the world, I would forever hear the negativity of my stepmother asking how I was going to be a father? How was I going to share with any child in my care how I was not their actual father?

I realized it wasn't much different than a child that had been adopted. So after having my personal pity party, I got my mind together and kept on pushing toward my goals.

8

SINGLE AGAIN... FOREVER

Well, it was back to being me. I was alone for the first time in a long while. This alone time allowed me to dig deeper into who I was becoming. We all go through changes in life, and we shift in the direction we need to reach our goals. I had to reassess what my goals actually were. What did I think success meant and how was I going to become successful?

Being able to take care of myself financially was the biggest point, in my opinion, of what success looks like. I slowly started to realize success and having money weren't the same. I was single, I had no real responsibilities except for me. My son was now living with his mom and I would visit and meet with him, but he didn't stay with me often. It took a lot of growing up for my ex and I to reach a common ground with him. I still would provide and help with him, and since he didn't live with me, my direct responsibility was decreased.

Once again, I buried myself in my job. I started learning how to get into different systems and how to make our location better. I looked more into what it meant to be a manager within the company and started driving hard at that goal. Although my manager had told me that I didn't want to do that, I told him he couldn't tell me what I wanted to do. I found different managers in the company to help me through the process of learning more and preparing my mind to move into that position.

My manager changed and so did so many people's attitudes at the location. Our new manager had such a positive outlook on how things were, and he was a breath of fresh air. He was also a black man. Most of our shift was black employees and had only seen white people in positions of leadership. This was eye-opening to me and the boost I needed.

When I told him that I was interested in management and training, he was on it! I would meet with him and he would teach me some of the things he had learned since being a manager. One critical step he told me about is hearing what the other employees wanted. In my position, I was already a baseline supervisor. There were four of us who directed the other employees to get things done in a safe and timely fashion.

I spoke with my colleagues and we decided to have a meeting every Friday with the team. Friday was typically a slower day for us, so it would work out pretty good. We started by answering questions that the employees had. Questions such as how to make the shift smoother? Who wanted to learn more about the details of the operation, as well as who wanted to simply come to work and leave? These meetings gave us all a better understanding of what each employee wanted. It also gave us a chance to teach them some things.

I was into the numbers of the operation so I started teaching numbers. The cost of employees staying on the clock too long, how much our customers pay for shipping, and why it's important to take care of their packages.

As time went on, we eventually got another manager and she was about business. Within only a few months of her being there, she started me in the training program. We had conversations about my career and while I had been fighting trying to decide if I wanted to be a manager or in training, she told me I could do both. Every department had managers, so it didn't make sense to only focus on one path.

Meanwhile, in my personal life, I was living it up. I had a new car, well, it was new to me, and I drove up and down the East Coast! I would get together with my fraternity friends and we would go visit each other in different states. We celebrated birthdays, anniversaries, and pretty much anything that called for a gathering. I was loving all the bonding time that we were having. I was no longer depressed and didn't have to worry about over drinking. After getting myself together while living at Ms. Courtenay's, I knew how to control myself. Uber and Lyft were becoming more popular as well, so I had no excuse to drive if I felt I had too much to drink.

I was confident in myself and wasn't worried about how others' saw me in my skin. I didn't care that I still had a touch of feminism about me, especially when I was with a group of people who knew me for years. People who didn't know me made assumptions that I was gay, and I didn't care because I knew who I was. I started hooking up with people that I met online. I wasn't worried about a long-term relationship because I knew that's not what I wanted.

I was living life like I should have been had I gone to a regular college. But I had more life experience and more control. I even tried to hang out with my new coworkers, but that didn't last long. I maybe went out with them three times before I realized that wasn't the crowd for me. I didn't have any hard feelings about it. However, there seemed to be some judgment on their end.

As I was trying to move up, many started telling me I thought I was better than everyone else. It was as if they weren't used to seeing people want to move up and be successful in their own lives. I began to distance myself, which didn't help their perception. I knew where I wanted to be, and I knew how I thought I'd get there. I kept pushing.

I was still going to church. I wasn't going to an Episcopal church anymore, I attended a United Church of Christ. This church was an open and affirming church, which translates into LGBTQ+ friendly. I was able to be myself at this church. I had been going here since before my transition and continued going after. I even had a support group that I was asked to run by the pastor for other members of the transgender community. I didn't know how I could help, but to me, when someone of the cloth asks you to do something, and you are able, you do it.

One day, a long-standing member of the church asked me if I was seeing anyone? She had seen me through all of my adult relationships and watched me transition. I had seen her in the church for all these years, and never had a serious conversation with her. For her to ask me if I was seeing anyone threw me off. She was in a relationship with someone, so I wasn't sure where she was going with this conversation. I told her I was single, but I wasn't looking for a relationship. She said okay, but continued by saying she wanted me to meet someone.

I didn't want to meet anyone. I wanted to stay single and not worry about adding other people into my life. I didn't want to focus on how to please someone else. I was going to be a bachelor forever and have fun, casual relationships.

All of that changed when I finally met this woman named Tamara Joseph from the United Kingdom. I didn't go out of my way to meet her. We had a major pillar in the church pass away so we ended up meeting at her memorial. We started a great friendship and got to know each other. I asked her what she was looking for and she said a relationship. I told her I was not looking for a relationship, so if she found that somewhere, I understood if we couldn't be friends with benefits any more. We both were realists. There was no need to sugar coat anything. We began our casual relationship. We had no titles, and weren't official or anything, simply a call or text away if needed.

9

CHECKING ALL THE BOXES

I was working three jobs, talking to two women, and enjoying life. There started to be a lot of mention of transgender people in the world. Celebrity's children, and other actors and actresses who identified as transgender. I learned more about what it meant to be visible in the community. I started attending different meetings and rallies in the area. The first time I went to a Transgender Day of Remembrance event it was at the SC State House. Transgender Day of Remembrance is a day to memorialize those within the transgender community that have been murdered because of hate. I asked Tamara to go with me.

 Because of her previous living situation, she had been living with me for a few months. She was a paramedic and got hurt on the job. In a way, we had something in common. Both of us were first responders whose careers ended too soon by no fault of our own. I felt empathy for her and when she asked me if she could rent a room from me? I said, "Yes." There was no reason not to rent out a room, I was still in this three-bedroom house alone. The extra rent money would come in handy. Because of my previous issues with my mortgage, the payment was down tremendously, so I didn't worry about making money off of her.

She decided to go to the event with me. I also invited a few friends from the fraternity to go as well. My friends did show up, but because it was so cold, they left early. Not Tamara. She stayed with me, outside in the cold, literally shivering. I learned two important things about her that night. She hates being cold and she stands by her word.

After we left the State House, we walked to a restaurant where everyone met for an after gathering. We mixed and mingled, had some margaritas, and enjoyed each other's company. I gave her my jacket as we walked back to the car and it hit me like a ton of bricks. Love. I asked her right there, before we even got back into the car if she would be my girlfriend.

It threw me off because she said she had to think about it. We had been living together for a few months, what was there to think about? A lot actually. She had to think about what it meant to be in a relationship with someone who said they didn't want a relationship. Someone who was taking care of another man's child. Someone who was starting to become an activist and be seen more publicly. So I waited for what seemed like forever. Finally, she said yes and we were officially dating. She said yes again and we were married within 2 years.

During this time, there was a major push by conservatives to create what was known as the "Bathroom Bill" all over the country. The various bills stated that a person should use the bathroom that matches their assigned sex at birth or the birth that is listed on their birth certificate.

This is when my role in activism truly stepped up. Here in South Carolina, a group of transgender leaders created a messaging board where we kept up with hearings and other events happening. I was asked to speak during one of the hearings to show the diversity of transgender people. The idea that transgender was only male to female, or as folks disrespectfully would say, a man in a dress, was the only concept people had.

People were saying cruel things like "I don't want my daughter to see a penis in the bathroom" or "Perverts will say they are transgender so they can rape women in the bathroom." I didn't, and still don't, like the idea of people using children in the explanation of adult perversions.

I don't remember everything I said at the hearing. What I do remember is looking at the senator who presented this bill right in the eye and asking, "Do you want me in the bathroom with your wife?" He turned so red and I could tell he didn't think of this bill from the female to male perspective.

After this hearing, I was approached by the Executive Director for South Carolina Equality. We set up a lunch date to talk about me joining the board and chairing the TransAction Task Force. As my life was taking this turn into a full-on activist, I was excited for this opportunity. I was also aware that I was a token and I didn't want to tiptoe around that.

For those who don't know, a token is often a word used to describe when someone is hired to meet some sort of racial or gender quota. I asked the director what made me such a great candidate to be on the board and after some generic fluff about how well I speak, he finally admitted it. "Greg I'm an old white gay man, I can't begin to understand what the black or transgender community needs from our organization." Once this was admitted I knew there was work to be done and I felt valued. I traveled around the state speaking to various organizations about what it was like to be transgender and how it was to transition while on the job. I spoke at correctional facilities, other board meetings, and even some one-on-one specific meetings.

I was learning that many people were actually trying to improve their knowledge of the transgender community. Even more importantly, employers were trying to create safer workspaces. I also learned there was still a lot of work to be done. I wanted to take my opportunity as a black trans man to speak up on as many issues as possible. Although so much of what I spoke on was regarding my transition itself and what it was like, I always spoke about the layers of oppression.

I acknowledged that being a man actually gave me an advantage in some spaces. However, being a Black man was a disadvantage in the world, a part of transitioning I had never thought about.

Oftentimes people would ask questions about surgeries and religious beliefs in government spaces. It was mind-blowing when I couldn't get someone to understand these questions were inappropriate. When I'm speaking to a group of nurses, doctors, or mental health specialists, and the questions asked are 'What size is your penis?' or 'How did you grow a beard?' it worried me. How can you not think outside the binary? How can you seriously ask someone about their genitalia and not see how that is offensive? Although I was speaking in many places, I still had to be mindful I was representing another organization.

I had to learn how to maneuver in public spaces that I was granted access to by being in this position. One thing I knew I wasn't good at was acting like a politician. I could put on the face easily, smile, and shake hands, that sort of thing. But when it came to filtering what I said to make sure it was in line with the organization I was with, that's where I had the problem.

I worked hard to make sure what I said was not only my opinion but things that were best for those learning about transgender issues. The more places I visited, the more people wanted me to join their boards or programs. There was this urge to have transgender voices heard, and I was quickly being shuffled around to many organizations. This urge was driven by grant money, which I later understood.

I did many lunch and learn events, where I was the only speaker, or panelist, answering questions regarding transgender issues. Then came the fight for me to help within the HIV/AIDS activism world. This is when I started to work with Dr. Bambi Gaddist, an activist who's been doing work within this field since about 1985. She was even once coined as "the AIDS lady". As new medicines were being discovered more funding was available for organizations that had programs involving transgender people. While there were several people that could have been involved, many people did not feel safe to be out. As someone who had already lost my career and coming into my own realization of who I was in regard to activism, I was being stretched very thin!

I started to notice there were more conversations needed. There was physical work that could be done to help the transgender community. I started thinking of the help I didn't have when I started my transition. I wanted to make a difference in people's lives, their everyday lives, not only in educating the public or workforce.

As I presented many of my ideas to the organizations I was involved in, I realized each already had very specific goals and plans in mind. SC Equality was focused on policies that were inclusive throughout the state, which is something that was, and still is needed. However, I felt as if there was something missing.

This is when I knew I would have to create what I was imagining. I had to find a way to reach the community right where they were. I began to work on building my own organization. Working out my mission and my vision, figuring out how I was going to help the transgender community. I thought about my own journey, what I had easy access to, what I didn't know about, and where I had to go to get things done.

I wanted to keep things as basic as possible. I knew I wasn't in a place to help people with gender-affirming surgeries. There weren't doctors in the state doing any of these surgeries so that wasn't going to be a direction I went. I chose to get better at court documents and find a way to help transgender folks navigate through their daily spaces.

10

MY OWN SPACE

I knew the work I wanted to accomplish would take more than me. I knew that it would take more than transgender folks to reach the masses. I began seeing a different doctor because I heard the facility was doing work in the transgender community. During one of my visits, I met a therapist, Suzanne, who was working with transgender clients to give them a more holistic approach in one place.

I wasn't sure how to approach her, or what to say. I knew I wanted to tell her about the work I was doing, as well as about the ideas for the future that I had. This wouldn't be my first time explaining and hoping to get help, but I wanted it to be fruitful. Apparently, someone told her a little about the work I was already doing so I didn't have to say much. She sat down beside me and opened up about what she was doing, and how she envisioned helping the community. We immediately connected. I could tell she was genuine in her work, and she saw my vision becoming a reality.

At this point I was still working at the shipping company, so that is where much of my time was spent. Outside of the job, I was pushing activism, recognition, and awareness about transgender issues. My speaking engagements continued to pick up, to the point that I was actually taking time off work to make sure I could attend. I looked into the LGBT organization within the company, but it was not organized. I figured if I could be an activist within the job, it would be a win for me. I couldn't get an answer fast enough, my fire was moving and I didn't want to be stopped. I took that dive into creating my own not for profit organization, with the intention of becoming an official 501c3 non-profit. I began to look for grassroots grants, ask for donations on Facebook, and host fundraising events.

Suzanne became a major motivator for me to keep pushing for my dreams. She became a guide for me on how to reach people, how to get what I need, and how to get a seat at the table. Dr. Gaddist made sure I understood not just any seat, a paid seat. I reached out to another grassroots organization in the Upstate area of South Carolina- Gender Benders. They were having so much success in providing support and resources to the community, I wanted to be connected with them in any way and still keep the brand that I was building. I wasn't sure this was possible, I had already been in several situations where I was asked for my thoughts, told the organization didn't have money to actually pay me, then never contacted again.

This organization wasn't like that. In fact, they encouraged me to continue my brand and said it was okay for me to adopt their processes. I was able to hold a name change clinic, which was the focus of my organization. While a name change is such a simple process, especially in South Carolina, it can come with much hassle when it's for someone who identifies as transgender.

The first clinic I had, Suzanne let me use her office, and Gender Benders had two representatives come and guide me through the process. There were six people at that first clinic. We walked through every page of the application and were able to give a stipend to help offset the cost.

I was so proud! I knew this is what I was supposed to be doing. I finally found what made me feel good, which made me happy. I continued to get donations and began to use my connections as a former police officer to help get forms done.

Tamara and I were doing well. She was well aware that I was moving fast in this activism lane, and she was so supportive. We began to have a conversation about me leaving my full time job at the shipping company. How would that look? What we would do for finances? You know the normal conversations you have when you're going to leave a job. However, I was too afraid. So I continued to try and balance a job with the work I was doing.

I started correcting people at the job. As conversations came up about LGBTQ+ issues, I would stop them and refocus the conversation on what was more work appropriate. Although I hadn't told my coworkers that I was transgender, I know they knew. My Facebook page was public and filled with all the work I was doing. I never considered myself stealth, or hidden, I just chose for it to be on a need to know basis. I had already lost one career, I didn't want to risk it again.

The more involved I got, the more I wanted to help. What started as a mission to assist people with getting name changes, evolved into helping getting gender marker changes, finding doctors, therapists, surgeons, and whatever someone would ask me for that I thought I could get. I finally had the same feeling I had when I was policing. That sense of helping others has always been a part of who I am, and it was back!

The help I was giving was a lot of one-on-one help through word of mouth. I was working on how to actually build my brand and build trust within the community. There were people who didn't want to see me succeed. When their voice got louder, I knew that meant I was on the right path.

Everything around me seemed to be improving and advancing rapidly. Then one day, Tamara got a phone call about her mother. Her mom was in the hospital in New York and she needed to get to her. After being away for about three weeks, I was able to take time off work and go to New York and help her work things out. We found out her mother had dementia, later diagnosed as Alzheimer's. I knew she couldn't stay alone. So we packed up what we could, got my mother-in-law, and her three dogs, and drove back home.

Neither of us knew much about Alzheimer's and what it would be like to be caregivers for someone dealing with this disease. It changed our world. I was still able to do activist things, but usually, her mom was with me, somewhere sitting in the audience observing. She enjoyed watching me speak, so it was easy to keep her entertained.

We quickly learned about Sundowners. This is when there is a heightened sense of confusion and anxiety in the late afternoon or evening in Alzheimer's patients. The problem I was having is that this would occur while I was at work. During the day I was the voice of reason. I had no previous emotional connections to my mother-in-law, so it was easy for me to joke and calm her when it was needed. Tamara, on the other hand, was having a hard time dealing with the emotional roller coaster that comes with taking care of a parent. I felt that I needed to step up in caring for my house. My family needed me.

I spoke to my boss on how to make sure that my job would be secure if I took a leave of absence. I looked up company policy and filled out a few forms, but I couldn't get the time off that I needed. Tamara and I spoke again about the idea of me leaving the job. We wrote out a plan, the benefits, the disadvantages, and what our fears were. We spoke on how we wouldn't let our fears win. I had lost a job before with no plan. This time I decided to leave a job, on my terms, with a plan in hand.

I left the company. I felt like the weight of the world was lifted off my shoulders. All the connections I made over the years there, all the managers I had reached out to while trying to further my career, all the trainers that I had worked with, were now-former coworkers.

To my surprise, not one single person contacted me to ask why I left, not even an exit interview. This lack of concern for how a dedicated employee could just leave, without any questions, let me know, I made the right decision. And to be honest, it hurt my feelings.

Now, I had all the time I needed to focus on building my brand. I had more one-on-one meetings, spoke to more doctors, educators, prison employees, and everyone ready to learn about what it meant to be transgender. People were ready to acknowledge they had transgender clients or patients and wanted to find the best ways to serve them.

I was beginning to truly build a reputation. Transgender people were coming to me more and more for help. I connected people with new Hormone Replacement doctors, Primary Care Doctors, Therapists, and jobs. I looked for where folks were already comfortably working and tried to get others there. My voice became much more valuable than I imagined it would be. Getting paid to share my story, to tell my personal journey, was like a dream come true.

As I continued to get invited into spaces to share my knowledge, I also continued to invite others who had stories. While I was learning the power of my story, I understood everyone's experience was different and equally as valuable. I was able to reach out to others within the fraternity as well to help me with branding, sharing ideas, concepts, and creating my website.

I had to work hard to balance my life as an activist and as a husband. Of all that was going on, this was probably the hardest because for some reason some things didn't seem to come naturally. Tamara was, and is, the best thing to happen to my life. She gave me the courage to do exactly what I was doing. She has supported me in every way she knew how, and I had to be sure to do the same. Free time from a regular job gave us time to build a better relationship. Only having been married for two years before her mother moved in was straining, but we made it work.

We made the decision to be happy in all that we do. That doesn't mean everything was perfect, it means we worked on us to keep our lives as peaceful and happy as possible. We used our past experiences to build up who we were individually and as a couple. Our openness to talk about the tough issues, guided us to be stronger and wiser together. We had the audacity to be genuine and true.

Epilogue

At the time this book was written the world was experiencing a shift. The pandemic known as Covid-19, or the Coronavirus, was taking over. It was as if a line was drawn and people were in a state of mass panic, or simply not caring. Many countries took a shut down approach to keep people away from each other and to keep infection rates to a minimum.

The United States let each state decide it's fate, which led to more being infected with the virus as well as more deaths. Stores ran out of disinfectant items, toilet paper, and food shelves were bare. People lost jobs, kids were out of school, and families were stuck at home with each other.

The United States has always had inequality when it came to minority groups, indigenous people, women, and people of color. As an activist, I've often had to be "more" trans than black in some situations, and "more" black than trans in other situations. While everyone was stuck home trying to quarantine due to this pandemic, a murder happened. This murder was televised.

A police officer murdered a man named George Floyd. This wasn't the first video of a black man being murdered by police officers, but this was a major catalyst in the fight for justice and equality. A young lady named Breonna Taylor was also murdered by police, while she was asleep in her own home. As of yet, there has been no arrest or video release of this incident.

People took to the streets protesting. Not only in America, but in other countries as well. Politics were involved in every angle of how this situation was going to be dealt with. Videos of more murders by police officers, more corrupt and inept police officers, were popping up. Older cases were being opened. The fight for civil rights was boosted. People, all people, were hearing what was true and real for Black people. Civil War statues were coming down, buildings were being renamed, and national sports teams were changing their names.

There were peaceful protests met with tear gas and rubber bullets. People infiltrated these protests to create riots and looting, trying to change the narrative of why people were protesting. People were exhausted. People were realizing how the past was truly affecting day-to-day life for minorities. The world was acknowledging systemic racism in the United States as a real thing. Of course, everyone didn't agree, but there were more people willing to have the conversation.

Then, a great leader in the Civil Rights Movement died, John Lewis. A man who never stopped working for civil rights and whose story is still motivating young people to be involved with the right thing. His death created a renewed sense of motivation for me, for my family, to keep doing what we were doing, pushing for equality, equity, and inclusion.